Bolsover Now and Then

by

Bernard Haigh and Geoff Harris

Published by Silver Press

First published 2010

© Copyright Bernard Haigh and Geoff Harris

Published by Silver Press
Archbishop School House, Main Street, Warton, Carnforth, LA5 9PG
Email: info@silverpress.co.uk

ISBN: 978-0-9567132-0-9

Design by Geoff Harris

Printed in Swansea by Harcourt Litho Ltd

Front cover: Scarcliffe Nurseries and Flecknell's butchers in Market Place 2010 and circa 1906.
Rear cover: Bolsover Parish Church 2010 and 1960.

Foreword by Dennis Skinner MP

I have lived long enough to remember the old pictures of Bolsover that are displayed in this splendid new book.

As a young miner I came to the Sportsdrome to see Bruce Woodcock. On our bus was a Clay Cross character, Stocky Phipps. He confronted Woodcock, the ex heavyweight champion, with the words "I've put down bigger men than thee". Bruce threatened to come round the bar. He was fuming when one of our group said, "It's a joke - Stocky's the local gravedigger!"

Yes, memories are wonderful reminders of how we lived and that is why this book is so important to the town and its people.

For forty years I have been proud to represent the constituency of Bolsover and during that time I have communicated with thousands of its people every year.

Now, together we must regenerate the area by providing new employment. That is why I fought to secure a Bolsover junction on the M1, clean up the pit tips and Coalite to provide land for jobs for 8000 men and women.

And then someone in the future will look at fresh photos, new buildings and above all memories that remind them of another remarkable chapter in the life of this historic town.

Introduction

"Why on earth are we visiting Bolsover" the husband of the secretary of the visiting local history society asked of his wife who had organised the exchange visit." Surely, it's only a dirty pit town". Two hours later that same, very surprised and indeed rather brave man admitted to me his earlier fears." I'm amazed at what you have shown us, the centre could be somewhere in the Cotswolds."

Once again, to the outsider, Bolsover had demonstrated that 'former mining town' does not have to mean an automatic write off of all that is interesting, handsome of appearance and unworthy of a second glance. Fortunately, the town starts with the distinct advantage of an impeccable pre mining legacy, with buildings which may be seen on William Senior's town survey of 1634 still contributing to the present day Market Place. The street pattern of Cotton Street, Town End, Church Street, Middle Street and High Street was laid down by William Peveril in the Middle Ages This makes Bolsover, along with Castleton, the earliest planned town in Derbyshire. Three centuries later, William Cavendish's extravagant castle gave us a building unique in English country house architecture. Even the mining period threw up the gem of New Bolsover, one of this country's few examples of colliery model village developments. Over one hundred years after its conception its unity and its situation, sheltering below the castle in a rural and relatively unspoilt setting can still make you stand, stare and admire.

However, inevitably changes to the appearance of the town have occurred over the years, the majority of these being positive, yet some giving cause for regret. In the 1950's High Street offered a fairly complete picture of Georgian and early Victorian houses and cottages, a seventeenth century chapel and an exquisite farm house, its western end culminating with a striking mock Regency gothic house. Today, only a handful of these remain. Likewise, today's conservation area contained many eighteenth century cottages, few of which survived the demolition hammer. In retrospect of course, there was little choice, no government restoration or conservation grants then and many properties were insanitary and multi occupied. The climate of the time was not right. Renewal, not restoration, was the post war call.

In the past twenty five years I have written many books and guides to town and colliery but one project remained outstanding. This was to chronicle the changes of the past fifty years and show to outsiders and indeed to remind ourselves what a gem of a place we have to be proud of.

However, previous books had virtually exhausted old photo collections and I had no wish to recycle them. The opportunity came when John Middleton, Bolsover born and bred, former deputy head of New Bolsover school and founder member and president of Bolsover Camera Club presented me with a stack of negatives of the town he had taken in the 1950's and 60's, a time of great change. In some cases the photos were taken literally at the time of demolition itself, with piles of bricks and stones lining Cotton Street or Middle Street, with only the central roadway marking the fact that they were streets at all. Using many of John's negatives it has been possible to show the town as it was within living memory and on the cusp of change.

To complement the old I wanted not only someone who could do justice photographically to the Bolsover of today but who had a feel for the town. Geoff Harris, a professional photographer who has been visiting and photographing Bolsover for over twenty years, has these attributes. Geoff's photographs combine the necessary care and an eye for design in merging the old with the new so that the result, I feel, is way beyond what I originally believed possible.

Common to all former industrial communities Bolsover is not secure in its future. Life after coal is far from certain even twenty years following the end of deep mining in north Derbyshire. The economic base remains fragile. Much has been achieved, not least 'Skinner's Junction' M1 29A, offering the town fast communication links together with improved opportunities relating to markets and goods, tourism, commuting and employment. However, as with communities countrywide residents can make their own contribution to a town's rejuvenation. If town centres such as seen in these photographs are to survive, thrive and develop we need to actively support those local retailers, businesses and services based in them. Without us they close down, the local market place dies and we are all the poorer for it.

I hope you will agree as you scan this book that, in Bolsover, we have much to be proud of. Wherever it might be we are all guilty of taking for granted where we live. Sometimes we need to look afresh at what we have. Perhaps we need to talk the place up to each other and to outsiders. I trust what you see here will help you believe Bolsover is worth it.

Bernard Haigh
Bolsover
2010

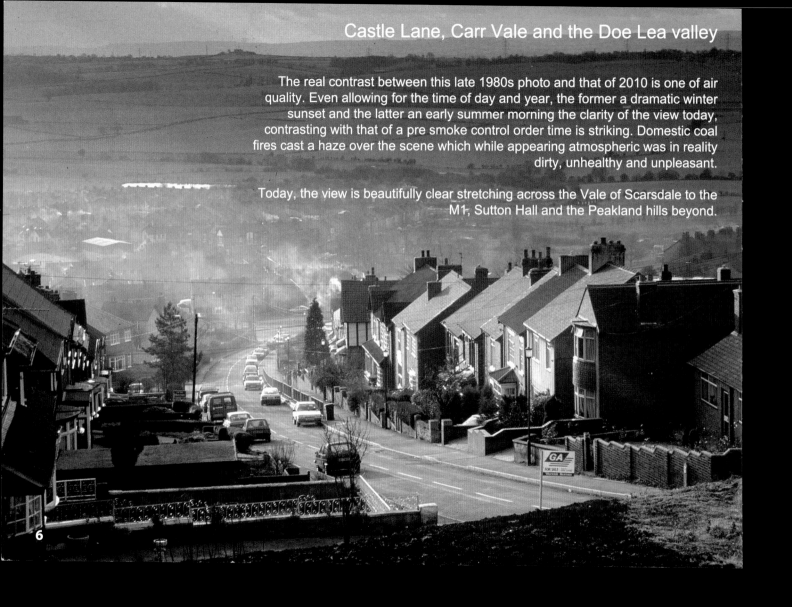

The real contrast between this late 1980s photo and that of 2010 is one of air quality. Even allowing for the time of day and year, the former a dramatic winter sunset and the latter an early summer morning the clarity of the view today, contrasting with that of a pre smoke control order time is striking. Domestic coal fires cast a haze over the scene which while appearing atmospheric was in reality dirty, unhealthy and unpleasant.

Today, the view is beautifully clear stretching across the Vale of Scarsdale to the M1, Sutton Hall and the Peakland hills beyond.

High Street in the 1920's

This appears to be a sleepy summer's day scene, taken around 1922. To the left of the recognisable Blue Bell, very much the hostelry at the heart of the old village, stood number 59, home of Mr and Mrs George Twidle. From here William Twidle kept a garage and ran his bus service to Shirebrook.

High Street keeps its stone built pre colliery identity fairly intact here although red brick cottages intrude to the left. On the parish church side of the road runs a harmonious line of magnesian limestone cottages punctuated only by the wall of the tithe barn. The sleepy looking road leads to St Mary's House at its western end.

No doubt the owner of the cart is quite sensibly slaking his thirst in the Bell.

Less complete than in 1922 many of the larger houses to the left and the majority of those on the parish church side were demolished fifty years ago. St Bernadette's Catholic church stands on the garage site and its adjoining barn has been converted into a good looking house, its garden replacing the brick cottages, a real enhancement to this side of High Street.

Opposite, the street has more gaps, giving a more open feel than in 1922.

Bolsover Methodist Church

This Edwardian view of Bolsover Methodist church, taken from Castle Street across the Hockley valley was obviously a well publicised occasion. The whole of Hill Top appears to be lining the walls in front of the chapel.

Opened in 1897 at a cost of £3,500 the chapel was known as 'Sykes's cathedral' for obvious reasons. Built virtually in the front garden of Sherwood Lodge, glimpsed here, home of Abel and Florence Sykes the building is a fine architectural contribution to Bolsover and can be seen from various parts of the town.

Although taken almost one hundred years later the fact that the scene offers so little change is the most striking thing. The cottages are virtually unchanged, Sherwood Lodge has been eclipsed by its trees and the brek linking Chesterfield Road with Hill Top is more overgrown.

However, sharp eyed observers will see that this scene was not taken in 2010. There is no Sykes Room extension, erected in 1993 following the sale of the adjacent cottages which were given by Abel and Florence Sykes to the church as a thanksgiving for the safe return of their sons from the Great War. Tree growth at the Edwardian photographer's vantage point makes this scene impossible to replicate today.

'Cow Tail Row,' Hockley 1958 Going, Going ......

Known locally as 'Cow Tail Row' these cottages backed into the hillside and stood between the barbers shop and the brek which runs between Station Road and Castle Street.

Anne Woodhouse remembered the residents popping in daily to her Market Place grocery shop for 'three penn'orth of pot herbs', comprising one carrot, a parsnip, an onion and a small turnip. Taken at the time of their demise in February 1958 the cottages up the brek were shortly to go also. The Sportsdrome can be seen top left.

….. Gone. A green oasis has replaced Cow Tail Row and effectively the town centre finishes here whereas until the 1950's Hockley was built up on both sides of the road with cottages, shops and a pub, the Nags Head, taking the urban core down to the Green at the junction of Station Road and Old Hill.

WELCOME TO BOLSOVER TOWN

13

Cotton Street looking towards High Street

In the mid 1960's Cotton Street became a bit of an urban wasteland. The site housing the lonely car will wait a full ten years for the new library, while opposite, space has been allocated for the car park. At the High Street end may be glimpsed the roof supports of the partially demolished tithe barn where in former days the agricultural tithe payable to the Duke of Portland was collected.

Across the road stands the then newly built Pentecostal church, an unhappy addition to High Street and few mourned its passing.

Cotton Street is obviously tidier than forty years ago and happily all the High Street buildings seen opposite remain.

More subtle changes include the Stubbins and Hope building, now converted from two cottages into one house, as has its neighbour to the right. The late Bunty and Charles Margerrison's house, perhaps the finest remaining example of Georgian domestic architecture in the town, is the least changed.

Charlesworth Street, Carr Vale

This beautifully evocative scene takes in Charlesworth Street and some of its younger inhabitants. Pinafores for every female in sight are obviously the order of the day, indicating that domestic work was heavy, laborious and often dirty. Washing by hand was a cumbersome chore and ironing with flat irons heated on the fire hot and exhausting.

The carrier stands proudly by horse and cart with thumbs in jacket lapel, the stance every self respecting Edwardian gent adopted when a photographer was in sight and one which has almost died out.

The grocery shop is now a deli and café and the symmetry of the two houses alongside, with the insertion of picture windows and new door openings, has gone. However, the shop window appears to be fairly original.

The long terrace rows on this side of Charlesworth Street were built around 1903 by Bolsover Colliery Company as miners housing additional to the model village. The Company built similar rows in Sherwood Street and Scarsdale Street. Each had three bedrooms, the end one in the two storey extension.

The availability of gas lighting at the turn of the century meant that the reduction of natural light, resulting from these 'tunnel backs,' was no longer seen as a problem. Although built later than the Company's housing at New Bolsover they were smaller and not as well built.

The opposite side of Charlesworth Street was private speculative building.

Castle Lane towards High Street 1955

The curve at the top of Castle Lane as it merges with High Street and the higgledy piggledy cottages at the top. Originally a rough track leading from the town and castle to the valley Castle Lane was known locally as 'water lane' because of the streams that trickled down its rough surface.

Early development on this steep hill was restricted initially to cottages at the turn of the bend as they nestled underneath the castle. Little else followed until the pit arrived in 1889 and individual plots were sold, often to colliery officials, starting at the bottom in 1906. The right hand side was not built on until the 1930's.

Notice the grooved footpath and handrail, invaluable in icy weather.

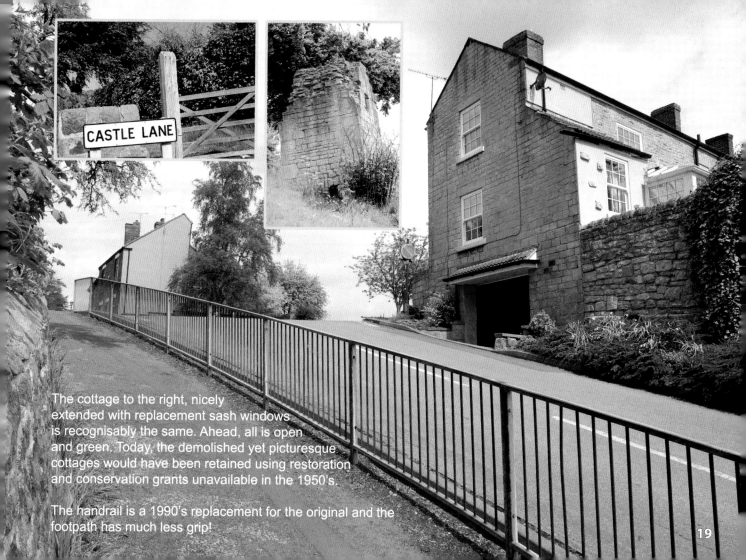

CASTLE LANE

The cottage to the right, nicely extended with replacement sash windows is recognisably the same. Ahead, all is open and green. Today, the demolished yet picturesque cottages would have been retained using restoration and conservation grants unavailable in the 1950's.

The handrail is a 1990's replacement for the original and the footpath has much less grip!

19

Church Street looking towards Cotton Street

15-19 Cotton Street is virtually all that remains south of Church Street, in this late 1960's scene. To the left sit the stone fronted cottages with brick to their backs, soon to go under the demolition hammer.

The cottages are late 17th century in date although probably remodelled with sash windows in 1762. Typical of a pre industrial Bolsover when the small town centre was a warren of such properties, their retention by a far sighted Urban District Council led by their Surveyor at the time, Charles Margerrison provides value to the townscape both architecturally and historically.

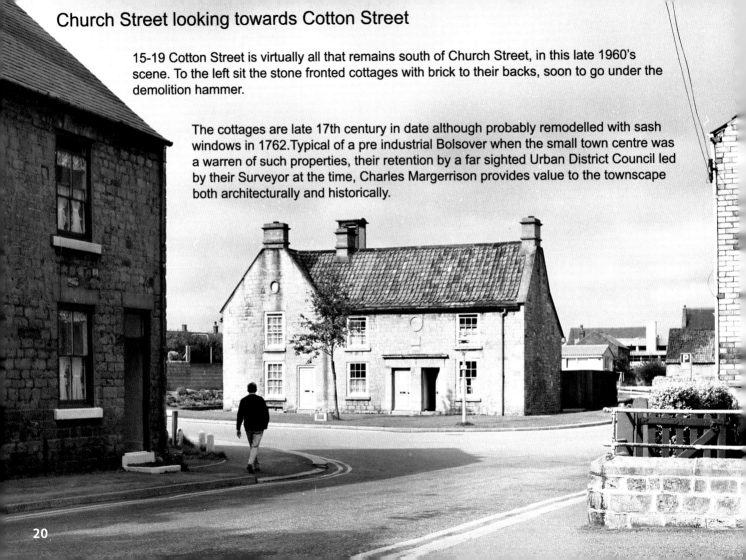

The Church Street building line now stands much further back, giving one side of the library a narrow north south frontage and widening the view up Cotton Street, towards the High Street fire station. The gas lamp in front of the cottages remains while its neighbouring sapling tree has matured nicely.

Cundy House

In the early 17th century, following the building of the castle, the problem of providing water to a building sited high on an escarpment full of rising spring water was solved by tapping into these same springs and conduiting it along lead pipes to the castle itself. Four of these stand on the hill to the south east of the castle and the fifth, popularly known as the 'Cundy House', stands to the north high above the Hockley valley and supplied water to the castle well house to the north of the keep.

This photo was taken in the 1980s when the Cundy House stood roofless, neglected and seemingly doomed to collapse.

In 2002 the Cundy House stands restored, following a long campaign by Bolsover Civic Society, who act as English Heritage appointed 'guardians' to ensure its ongoing maintenance. The building's rather sylvan and somewhat hidden situation helps protect it from vandalism.

Here we can see the new stone roof and gated opening leading to the internal well, built over a rising spring which was conduited across the Hockley valley to the well house. A gravity feed worked as the bottom of the castle well house was at the same height as the spring and water could be pumped to the top storey in order to feed the ornamental fountain.

The Cundy House was built around 1634 when William Cavendish entertained, at massive expense, King Charles I and Queen Henrietta Maria at Bolsover. Ben Jonson's masque 'Love's Welcome to Bolsover' was performed in the fountain garden with the audience seated on the walkway above.

Castle Street 1905

The gas lamp has replaced the original market cross, although the latter's stone base remains. This was the centre of the medieval town, directly facing the entrance gates to the first castle. To the left the brick building, in 1905 a butchers shop, has replaced an earlier stone agricultural building. The rest of this side of Castle Street is a combination of cottages, larger houses partially converted to shops and the boundary wall of the Congregational church.

The right hand side houses the Anchor and the original Angel. The parish pump, mid centre in front of the cottages, is a natural meeting place for the community as no doubt was the lamp standard for the Edwardian youth of 1905.

The cenotaph replaced the lamp standard in 1921 as a memorial to the fallen of the Great War. Unveiled by Mr. C.A. Cochrane, Chairman of the Bolsover Colliery Company. Designed by Sir Reginald Blomfield as the 'Cross of Sacrifice', erected in war cemeteries throughout northern France and Belgium, it is a fine memorial and lends dignity to the old Market Place.

To the left, the buildings from the 1905 photo remain unchanged although now wholly commercial in character. Opposite, the 'new' Angel, a handsome between the wars mock Tudor building has closed its doors as a pub and today houses the thriving Bolsover Antiques Centre. The Anchor is now partially rendered and the whole area semi pedestrianised.

THIS PUMP WAS ERECTED IN 2002 BY BOLSOVER CIVIC SOCIETY.

...PLACED

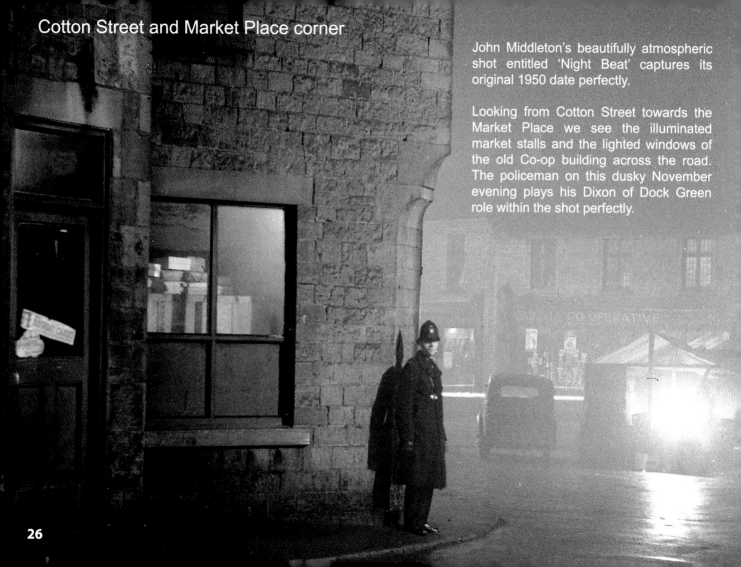

Cotton Street and Market Place corner

John Middleton's beautifully atmospheric shot entitled 'Night Beat' captures its original 1950 date perfectly.

Looking from Cotton Street towards the Market Place we see the illuminated market stalls and the lighted windows of the old Co-op building across the road. The policeman on this dusky November evening plays his Dixon of Dock Green role within the shot perfectly.

The indented stonework and windows are recognisably the same and the newly refurbished Cavendish dominates the Market Place. To its left the old Co-op has long gone … as has the new, to be replaced by the Factory Outlet Store.

Congregational Church, Castle Street

The late nineteenth century brought colliery prosperity and growth to the town. Many colliery officials and some miners were Congregationalist which tended to be a rather middle class face of nonconformity and a new church was erected in 1893 to the rear of the original chapel. Built by local builder William Cuttell of High Street with internal joinery by Mr. Handley, whose home and workshop were next door to the church, the new building with its small bell tower was an enhancement to Castle Street.

As was typical of the time, when much family life revolved around church or chapel, the 'Congs' was a thriving religious and social centre and nonconformists of all persuasions 'lived and died in the Lord'. Following the Second World War and old ties were gradually loosened its fortunes dipped and by 1980 the congregation totalled ten regular worshipers. The building was no longer viable.

Generations of Bolsover families; Flintofts, Shaws, Carringtons, Smiths, Hunts and Utridges were involved in the life of this building throughout its one hundred year history. Its demise symbolised the end of a way of life.

The medical centre does not possess the same presence as the previous occupant of the site but is not an unpleasant addition to the conservation area. Built in local magnesian limestone with pantiled roof it stands back within the chapel graveyard and walking past the dead is something Bolsover patients take very much in their stride.

In the graveyard is the commemorative stone to Christopher Hinde, Secretary to Bolsover Gas Works, Registrar, Chapel Deacon and Sunday School Superintendent. A Victorian pillar of the community par excellence.

The stone boundary wall is that of the original chapel and saved from demolition by Bolsover Civic Society.

Bolsover Colliery Club and Institute

The colliery club and institute is an attractive building which, in keeping with those other public buildings in the model village, Bainbridge Hall, the Stores and long demolished school, possesses a generalised arts and crafts feel.

A.W. Brewill was the Nottingham architect the Bolsover Colliery Company employed for the school and looking at the similarity in style it is likely he was also used for the Institute. Inside, it had a billiard room, reading room, smoking room, games room, committee room and a library of nine hundred volumes. There were five hundred members of the Institute which was the focal point of social activities in New Bolsover.

Externally the Institute has hardly changed and it remains a handsome building. Today, it is 'The Sportsman' pub, a radical change from the days of the Bolsover Colliery Company when they regulated the sale of liquor so that each man could be sold 'no more than three glasses between 6pm and 10pm'. Drunkeness was not the problem at Bolsover it could be at other pits, where the local coal owners exercised less control over their workforce, and absenteeism at Bolsover was 3% lower than elsewhere in the coalfield.

The Bowling Green in front and alongside it the cricket pitch were also provided by the Bolsover Colliery Company. As can be seen here both remain maintained and well used.

Cotton Street towards Church Street

A telling example of how even the smallest urban communities experienced wholesale demolition and renewal in the 1960's. Very little here in the process of demolition was worth keeping although the old cottage at the corner of Middle Street, here a pile of stones, may be a cause for regret.

Car parking space abounds…and it's still free forty years on.

Tidier, greener and cleaner with significant building changes. The rear of the library to the right and mid scene, beyond the flourishing WI tree, the gable end of Page's and the early 1970's block of shops which provide this side of lower Cotton Street with a good looking and attractive development.

The open market area, designed and opened by Charles Margerrison in 1973, perhaps in retrospect was not a good idea. The intention was to remove it from its untidy Kitchen Croft site where it had graduated when the Market Place was renovated in the early 1960's. Although a beautifully executed site markets are now seen as informal additions to the general street scene and it has returned to its original medieval position. The Cotton Street space awaits the developer.

Former Presbyterian Chapel, High Street

The old original Presbyterian chapel cannot be dated accurately but possibly was built in 1662 as a result of the Act of Uniformity of that year when two thousand clergy left the Church of England as a protest against prescribed worship following the Restoration of Charles II. Certainly it is one of the oldest non conformist chapel buildings in Derbyshire although there is no record of a regular congregation before the early 18th century. It became a Congregational chapel in 1813.

Beautifully crafted in hand made brick with stone dressing, in this scene it stands lost and rather unloved. The rear toilet block does not enhance.

Restored and standing proud 'The Old Meeting House' is now a private house. The rear outbuildings and toilets have mercifully gone, to be replaced by a well planted and paved garden.

The original building is revealed as the handsome addition to the street scene it is.

Market Place

Flecknell's butchers shop stood opposite the cenotaph. Originally called Fleischner he changed to the anglicised Flecknell during the Great War when anti German feeling was at its height. The enterprising butcher had a second shop at Carr Vale.

Today, Flecknell's premises houses children's wear. The building is one of the oldest in the town and is first shown on William Senior's estate survey for the Earl of Newcastle of 1634 when it would have been timber framed with cruck trusses. The whole range was refaced in magnesian limestone in the eighteenth century and following pressure from Bolsover Civic Society and the threat of demolition in 1979 the shops were beautifully restored by Derbyshire Historic Buildings Trust.

Although technically this shop sits next door to Flecknell's it is part of the original block and of exact appearance.

Scarcliffe Nurseries, with their colourful collection of fruit, vegetables and flowers, offer a positive enhancement to the Market Place scene, worthy of any tourist brochure. Here, Sylvia Lee and Avis Chapman display their wares and who could resist their colour and beauty?

Cotton Street 1968

Cotton Street is preparing for change but apart from the Trustee Savings Bank, built in the garden of what was Brayshaw's Decorators, little has happened as yet.

However, mid photo, above Church Street, things are moving and demolition is leaving gaps in the street line. Older readers will remember Weston's and the sweet shop to the left.

George's Fashions has replaced Weston's and the good looking parade of early 1970's shops to the right lead the eye up to the library and the top end of Cotton Street, an area of distinct change and improvement.

Bolsover Colliery from Hill Top

A panoramic view of that part of the Scarsdale valley which housed Bolsover Colliery, from the sinking of the shafts in 1889 to closure just over one hundred years later. The Coalite smokeless fuel and chemical plants stood adjacent, from 1937 until their demise a few years after the colliery.

In the foreground stands Castle Estate, an example of early post war public housing, in this case a joint scheme by Bolsover UDC and the Coal Industry Housing Association, the housing arm of the National Coal Board. The local authority housing was built by Wimpey using its no fines concrete system, an early post war pre fabricated system designed to satisfy housing needs as quickly as possible. Built to a confusing grid system along the steep slope below the escarpment it is unfortunate that the urgent post war housing needs did not lend themselves to more deliberation regarding siting and building materials.

The central part of the photograph is dominated by the colliery headstocks and pit buildings. The long row of offices to the left are the NCB headquarters of the North Derbyshire Area and Portland House, the original managers house built by the pre nationalised Company, may be seen gable end in the centre. Running along Buttermilk Lane with Duckmanton on the horizon, is the Coalite stockyard and the bulk of the colliery north tip.

The valley is cleaner, much greener and its industrial legacy, on the surface at least, has almost vanished. The colliery offices now form part of the Bolsover business park. To the top right the Coalite site remains a dreadful scar. Although cleared of buildings and coal stocks, apart from the sinister tank farm, it is an area of dereliction and contamination.

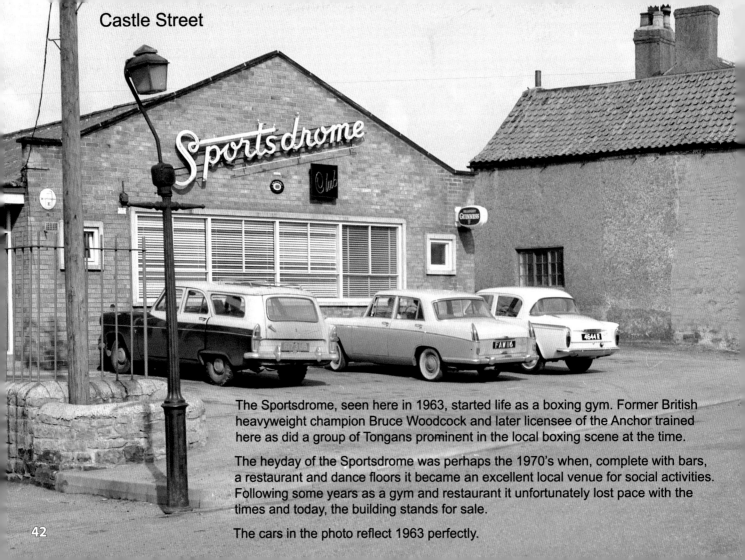

The Sportsdrome, seen here in 1963, started life as a boxing gym. Former British heavyweight champion Bruce Woodcock and later licensee of the Anchor trained here as did a group of Tongans prominent in the local boxing scene at the time.

The heyday of the Sportsdrome was perhaps the 1970's when, complete with bars, a restaurant and dance floors it became an excellent local venue for social activities. Following some years as a gym and restaurant it unfortunately lost pace with the times and today, the building stands for sale.

The cars in the photo reflect 1963 perfectly.

Hardly an improvement on its 1963 appearance the Sportsdrome's many additions and extensions over the years have only served to make it even less beautiful, Here we can see the original gable frontage with its blocked in windows has been flattened. Unfortunately, the building's restaurant glass frontage, overlooking the Hockley valley in order to catch the view, looks away from the town, which has to be content with its rear.

Following closure of the gym in 2009 it enjoyed a short spell as an Indian restaurant but major transformation work is needed if it is to have a future. Perhaps the time has come to call 'Time' on the Sportsdrome.

Designed in 1976 by Colin Fox of the County Council's architect's department Bolsover Library was one of the many replacements the council undertook in the 1970's.

The service began in Bolsover in 1932 in what is now the post office, transferring in 1948 to the Cotton Street council offices when Bolsover Urban District Council purchased Sherwood Lodge.

The first purpose built library in the town heralded a new dawn, embracing the new technology of the 1970's, a camera book issue system, seen here, and micro fiche catalogues.

Bolsover Library

A gramophone and tape lending service was introduced, an exhibitions area for art, photographic and community activities included in the layout and a branch of the East Midlands Tourist Board opened. The first floor housed meeting room and study area.

Two external views of Bolsover library taken twenty years apart. No dramatic changes; trees maturing from the earlier saplings, a seat commemorating councillor George Bratt, ramped access to the ground floor and raising of internal floor level to make this possible denoted by higher window level on ground floor far gable end.

This thirty five year old building is aging gracefully and remains perhaps the most handsome secular public building in the town and a credit to the county council.

High Street

This fine looking house belonged to, 'Cuthbert's, carters, haulage and hay factor'. Billy Cuthbert stands by the horse.

The business was one of a number of carters and haulage contractors who flourished in the town in the nineteenth and early twentieth centuries at a time when all businesses and farmers relied on horse drawn power. Others of note were Marsh's at Brown Dyke and Coupe's at Town End.

As motor transport slowly replaced the horse Billy Cuthbert went to work at Bolsover colliery as a coal carrier, still using horse and cart.

A fine line up of family members appear pleased to be photographed.

The Jehovah's Witness Hall is no real replacement for Cuthbert's but an improvement on the Pentecostal church which replaced the carter's premises. This flat roofed monstrosity of glass and painted wood cladding cried out to be demolished.

The present building, while lacking any pretence to architectural style, is built in local materials and the site is immaculately maintained.

Fidler's Rest, Old Hill

This building is early 19th century in origin and was built for his mother by Peter Fidler, surveyor, cartographer, trader and naturalist. Born in 1769 at Sutton Mill by the Doe Lea he entered the service of the Hudson Bay Company at the age of nineteen. Working his way up from labourer he acquired surveying experience and during the next thirty years journeyed throughout north west Canada, exploring and mapping previously unrecorded trade routes. He is credited with the first discovery of coal in western Canada. Fidler died at Fort Dauphin, Manitoba and is hailed as one of the country's founding fathers.

The original house was typically Georgian with the ground floor front extension added in the nineteenth century.

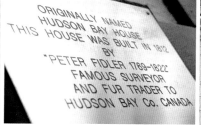

ORIGINALLY NAMED
HUDSON BAY HOUSE
THIS HOUSE WAS BUILT IN 1812
BY
"PETER FIDLER 1769-1822
FAMOUS SURVEYOR
AND FUR TRADER TO
HUDSON BAY Co. CANADA

Today, the pub commemorates Peter Fidler with a plaque placed jointly by Canadian members of the Fort Dauphin Museum, The Friends of Peter Fidler and his English descendents, notable of whom by marriage is Mary Fidler, who for over forty years has fought to have Fidler recognised in his native town.

The pub and restaurant has gone through a few name changes. For many years it was the Castle Inn but more recently it has been Hudson's, The Hudson Bay and now Fidler's Rest, each time commemorating its illustrious builder.

Marsh's farm, Hill Top and slightly to the left Hudson Bay Cottages, named after the great Canadian and trading company and in memory of Bolsover's famous son, Peter Fidler who was so instrumental in the late 18th century in opening up the vast Canadian wastes for the Company. The cottages were built above the house on Old Hill which Fidler had built for his mother.

Hill Top

Marsh's farm has been replaced by Hides Green, an early 1970's sheltered housing development built by Bolsover Urban District Council. This council had a very creditable housing record for a small local authority, stretching back to the 1920's when the Moor Lane estate was built, through to the 1960's and '70s when it concentrated on sheltered developments such as The Paddock and Orchard Close. Hides Green is perhaps the most successful, situated on a spacious well landscaped site with a relatively small number of dwellings to the acre.

The house to the right has shed its 1950's TV aerial and Hudson Bay Cottages are long gone.

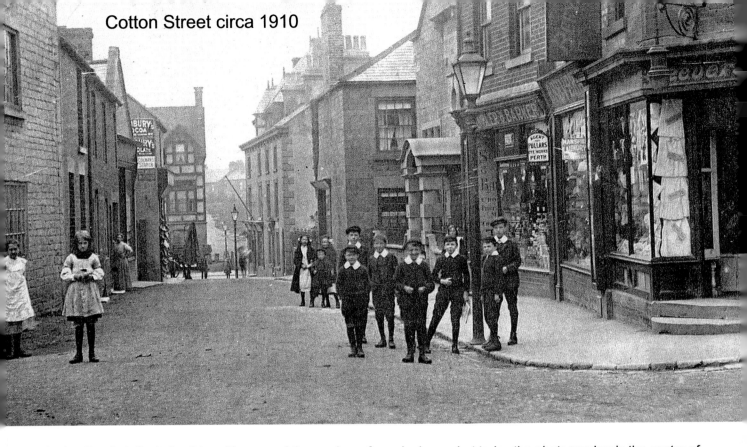

Cotton Street circa 1910

No doubt after dark the lads pictured here used the gas lamp for swinging on but today the photographer is the centre of attention. The smart Norfolk jackets, starched collars and caps would suggest a school day. Hopefully, some of these lads would survive the cataclysm of the Great War, a few years off.

Today's post office is here a draper, complete with handsome gas lamp and the house below the council offices was Brayshaw's decorators. To the side of the Cavendish a path leads through Kitchen Croft to Oxcroft Lane in the distance.

A more informal, brighter and comfortable school uniform is the order of the day but the children seen here still attend the same school as their 1910 forebears, although not the same building. Bolsover Church of England School has moved from its Castle Street site to Horsehead Lane.

Today, Brayshaw's is now a solicitors and decorating has moved across the road to Page's. The drapery shop entrance has been exchanged for a 'hole in the wall'.

High Street

This view of High Street shows a beautiful combination of cottages, Georgian and early Victorian houses, all providing a fine street scene, which at this time could give that Lincolnshire gem, Stamford, a run for its money.

The eastern end of High Street has been cleared of cottages to make way for garage and bungalow. Further along, some of the houses remain but changed in appearance. It is not until the Bell is reached in the far distance that High Street reclaims some of its value glimpsed in the previous photograph. However, as a whole, the street retains its wide and intermittently green attractiveness.

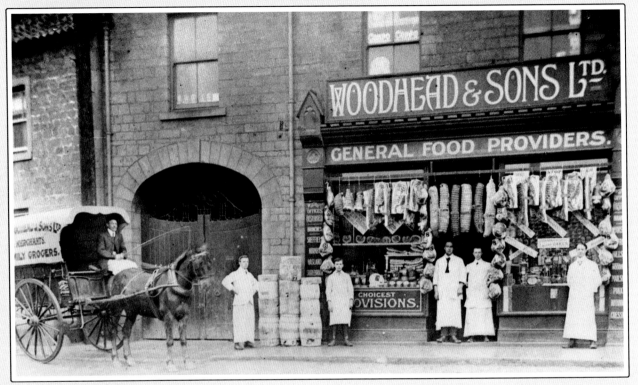

Woodhead and Sons had branches of its grocery shops throughout south Yorkshire and the north Midlands. The Bolsover branch stood centre of the Market Place, set back from the road. Here we see the manager and his assistants proudly displaying their wares. In those days before canned goods and frozen food most grocers weighed out individually. Some of us can remember butter sold in patted slabs and loose sugar poured into blue paper bags. You could even handle and select your Sunday joint from those on display outside the shop. The bluebottles and flies must have enjoyed a feast day!

Also pictured is Woodhead's carriers cart for home deliveries,
one hundred years before Tesco came up with the idea.

Farm Foods illustrates how shopping has changed for many people. Frozen, canned and pre packaged is the order of the day, however, the hygiene rules are probably an improvement. Woodhead's building was demolished in the 1960's but the design for the new one echoed the old, with a similar gabled first floor and sash windows. The adjacent building, now Dennis Riley's Electrical Store, is the same as in the previous scene.

If you are wondering what happened to the archway, well, today it stands opposite the post office, dividing Middle Street from Cotton Street.

Castle Street

A peaceful view of the three cottages standing alongside the entrance to the castle. The smaller one nearest the camera still has its Yorkshire sashes, sliding left to right, while the other two have the later vertical ones.

Unlike later houses in the town, which tended not to have cellars due to mining subsidence, these three had below ground accommodation going down into the pillar of rock which British Coal always insisted they left intact underneath the castle.

Picturesque they might look but the internal living conditions must have been primitive.

If conservation and restoration grants had existed at the time of demolition no doubt the cottages would have been enlarged and restored to form desirable residences. Today, the site, a hugely important one within the conservation area, is worthy of improvement.

PRIVATE PARKING CUSTOMERS ONLY

Town End 1963

All the buildings on the right hand side remain, some with new owners offering different goods. Albert Leaning started as an electrician at the pit and opened his first shop in the 1930's, selling home made crystal wireless sets from a small hut to the rear of his later business premises.

To the left the bay windowed houses adjoining the Plaza were demolished to make way for the Co-op supermarket development as was the cinema. The boys on their butcher's bikes seem to be making heavy weather of it!

Taken further along Town End this view includes one of the oldest buildings in the town, the stone and pantiled part cruck building which started out life as a pair of cottages and shop. Dating from the seventeenth century it is listed and today houses baby wear whereas in 1963 it was a grocer's. Note the first floor sliding sashes, still in place. Alan Harrison's jewellers shop remains a constant feature of Town End and Bert Leaning's was taken over by Frank Smith, one of Leaning's apprentices along with Dennis Riley, the latter still a valued Market Place retailer of electrical goods.

Hornscroft Road 1958

The solitary pedestrian walks
unconcernedly ahead of the lady cyclist,
no footpath yet and no worries about traffic volume.
Taken before Hornscroft Road was widened and the churchyard wall
removed further into the graveyard. The terrace to the right maintains
its original style, not a PVC window or door in sight.

HORNSCROFT ROAD

A much less sleepy feel pervades the current scene. A wider road with increased traffic creates a more urban feel today.

Limekiln Fields

Limekiln Fields originally formed part of Wood Field, which, together with Moor Field and Middle Field, comprised the large open field system of the Middle Ages, adjacent to the town. These were later divided up into strips for villagers to farm individually. The area became known as Limekiln Fields in 1780 as a result of limestone quarrying at nearby Shuttlewood, when stone was burnt to make lime to sweeten the clay soil of Shuttlewood Common.

The windmill seen here dates from 1793. The brick chimney is late nineteenth century when steam power replaced the sails to drive the corn grinding machinery. A second and later steam mill was Bagshaw's on Welbeck Road.

Does anyone recognise the little girl peeping over the gatepost?

The road is less rural, the house to the right has gone to make way for road widening and the terrace modernised. The mill field is now residential, while the mill, which is listed, graces a private garden as does the steam chimney behind.

To the right the row of bungalows sit in what until fairly recently was clearly recognisable as one of the medieval strips. These were allocated to villagers before the Bolsover Enclosure Act of 1780 enclosed Wood Field.

Bolsover Parish Church

The parish church suffered two major fires,
the first in 1897 and again sixty three years later.

This dramatic and rather sad snowy scene taken directly after the 1960 fire shows
the extent of the damage to the roof timbers and the main body of the building.
Miraculously, the thirteenth century tower and later broach spire remained intact. It
helped that the fire brigade could be summoned quickly, unlike 1897 when John
Bagshaw, an engineer on the Scarcliffe tunnel,
had to gallop ten miles on horseback to Welbeck
Abbey where the nearest fire appliance was stationed.

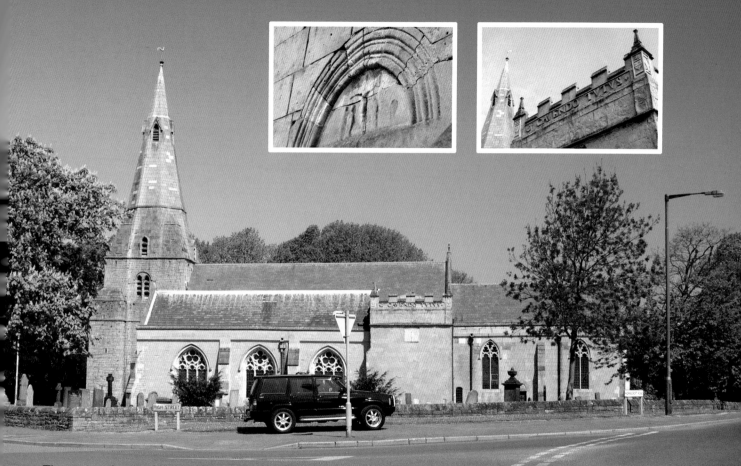

The restoration work undertaken by Taylor, Young and Partners included a new octagonal vestry to the north east side of the building. The Cavendish chapel was undamaged in the 1960 blaze and was used for services until the restoration was completed.

In this 2010 scene the 4X4 shows that it is not only the church which has been updated.

Town End Primitive Methodist Chapel 1966

Primitive Methodism began in Bolsover in what is now the Town
Council offices in Cotton Street and later, as the movement grew, into this fine
example of nineteenth century nonconformist architecture in the best no nonsense chapel tradition.

By the time this photo was taken in1966 the building was proving too large and expensive for a dwindling
congregation. It was demolished in 1974 and the 'Prims' merged with the Wesleyans at Trinity, to meet at Hill Top.

To the left of the chapel stands Bolsover clinic, also demolished, its services concentrated into the new adjoining
Health Centre.

Built to the same scale as the chapel, Pegasus Court is a residential development which in a strange way suits the site. Not too dissimilar in style but minus its predecessors Victorian confidence it is not a too unworthy successor.

Market Place and Cenotaph

The caption on the original print says 1930's but it is more likely ten years later, possibly war time, and will be familiar to anyone who remembers the town in the 1950's or early 60's as much of what can be seen here was still around then, and serving similar purposes.

The Westminster Bank on the corner was accommodated in Christopher Hinde's house and didn't remove to Cotton Street until the late 1970's. The house behind the cenotaph was Dr.Spencer's, later Kennington's the dentist. To the right Meadow Dairy was a grocer familiar throughout the land until thirty years ago. Hollingworth's fish and chip shop was an establishment known to many older inhabitants.

Only Greenwood's chemist, top left, has gone, but this unlovely red brick pile was a bit of an interloper in the magnesian limestone of the Market Place.

Hollingworth's old shop still sells fish and chips but enlarged premises now include café facilities. The dentist has given way to a thriving Italian restaurant, which ideally should set the tone for how to renovate commercial premises in the town and enhance the local street scene. The bank has transferred location, to be replaced by 'Needles and Pins' knitting and sewing shop.

Sixty years later the area has been pedestrianised and the cenotaph stands amid summer planting and protected by smart railings.

Sherwood Lodge

Built in 1897 for Abel Sykes, a director of the Bolsover Colliery Company, this was the largest occupied private house in the town. A large and rather unlovely Victorian villa, Sykes's granddaughter, in 1976, remembers the house 'with marble busts and potted ferns in the entrance lobby, leading towards stags heads and foxes masks in the hall'.

Sykes and his wife Florence lived in upper middle class style typical of the time, with four reception rooms including library and a sitting room containing gardening catalogues for Florence and copies of the *Methodist Recorder* for Abel. Outside, the house sat in sizeable wooded grounds and looked towards the chapel, funded by Sykes, with a rose garden where Florence would sit.

In 1948 Sherwood Lodge was sold to Bolsover UDC for use as council offices. The band stand was built in the early 1960's for the twinning ceremony with Decazeville, Bolsover's twin town in France. Joe Mason, council builder, remembers Charles Margerrison, town surveyor, requesting that the side pillars be built and demolished four times before he felt they were positioned correctly.

The integrity of the original building has gone, with its gradual enlargement for council purposes.

In 1974 when local government reorganisation merged Bolsover with Blackwell and Clowne Rural Districts, to form Bolsover District, the new council extended Sherwood Lodge with the central brick building, above. Twenty years later as central government looked at the feasibility of merging councils and losing a tier of local government Bolsover decided that it would have a better chance of survival if it based all its operations at its main centre of population and indeed in the correct county! It sold its Nottinghamshire offices and extended Sherwood Lodge.

This move was good for the town and its retailers, but as a building Sherwood Lodge lost its original presence.

Station Road 1953

The coronation festivities of 1953 were taken up with great enthusiasm by the country at large, welcomed by a war weary population still suffering the effects of food rationing, national shortages and the dreariness of the early 1950's. Bolsover was no exception and the excuse for a bit of fun, colour, bunting, flags and pageantry is evident in these window displays. It is hard to imagine a future coronation whipping up such levels of enthusiastic patriotism.

Shops and services have been replaced by offices, losing valuable retail space which could help the town regain some of its retail base.

When modernised in the 1990's the roof dormer windows were unfortunately removed thus reducing the impact of the building.

Looking towards the Market Place and along the north side of Town End all of this view remains intact, the main change being one of cottages into shops.

No building changes here, merely shop
windows where cottage sashes once were.
Extra room for pedestrians rather than cars
is the order of the day.

The phone box, one of Sir Giles Gilbert Scott's original designs,
is now listed, although in the era of mobile phones seldom used.

Ahead, the Cavendish sets the tone for good quality
refurbishment within the town centre.

77

Old Hill

Pre colliery cottages built for agricultural workers on Old Hill. Dressed stone frontages with rough cast gables and rear walls they comprised two bedrooms, a front parlour and rear scullery kitchen. Originally enjoying an enviable position looking directly on to the castle by the time this photograph was taken they were less open in outlook and their years numbered.

The motorcycle offers a slight touch of modernity.

Cottages have been exchanged for post war housing yet part of the original garden wall remains.

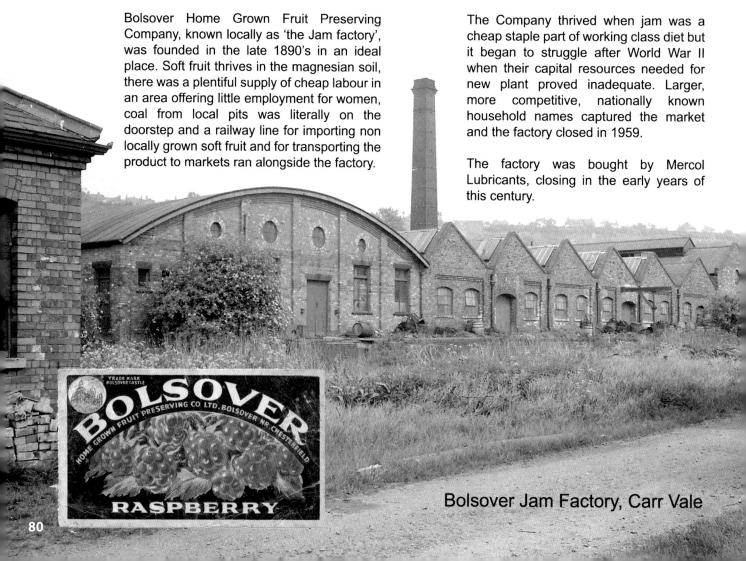

Bolsover Home Grown Fruit Preserving Company, known locally as 'the Jam factory', was founded in the late 1890's in an ideal place. Soft fruit thrives in the magnesian soil, there was a plentiful supply of cheap labour in an area offering little employment for women, coal from local pits was literally on the doorstep and a railway line for importing non locally grown soft fruit and for transporting the product to markets ran alongside the factory.

The Company thrived when jam was a cheap staple part of working class diet but it began to struggle after World War II when their capital resources needed for new plant proved inadequate. Larger, more competitive, nationally known household names captured the market and the factory closed in 1959.

The factory was bought by Mercol Lubricants, closing in the early years of this century.

Bolsover Jam Factory, Carr Vale

All evidence of the factory has gone and in its place a new housing development takes shape. Once completed this will finally link Bolsover and Carr Vale with continuous residential development, as the foot of the valley estate joins the new houses on the edge of Carr Vale. At its southern end the new development approaches the closed Scarcliffe tunnel.

Portland Crescent

In 1920 Bolsover Urban District Council commenced its house building programme, encouraged by the Housing and Planning Acts and the scarcity of 'Homes for Heroes' following the Great War.

The Moor Lane site was purchased in 1921, providing almost thirty acres, followed by a further eighteen before the outbreak of World War II. Housing for the elderly has always had some priority with the council and some of the earliest bungalows to be built in the town may be seen here during the course of construction. Portland Crescent offered one bedroomed semi detached dwellings built around a wide grassed area with deep front gardens, very much in the cottage style. Expensive in terms of land usage, today their place has been taken by sheltered housing units offering a more communal and possibly urban way of living.

Eighty years later the development has matured. Wood has given way to PVC and what is noticeable is the small number of properties an acre, something which current land values would make unlikely. This is emphasised with the open plan of the scheme. In the 1920's each bungalow was fenced off from the road and its neighbours, residents enjoying their own private garden. The fences for the whole estate were removed in the 1960's. Although convenient for contract grass cutting and easier for elderly residents to maintain, the retention of private gardens with fences and mature planting would have led to the realisation of a more intimate and private feel.

Middle Street is fast disappearing and John Middleton took this before almost every building had gone.

The only two shops remaining today on Middle Street itself are the flat roofed ones to the right. Today, they house a hair dresser and furniture shop. To the right of them may be seen the rear roofs of the Hair Studio and Scarcliffe Nurseries. Straight ahead is the rear bulk of Greenwood's Chemist, sitting in what today is Middle Street car park. The stone and pantiled building between the three storey one and those to the left in process of demolition is the former barn to the rear of Bella Blu.

Middle Street 1963

The only recognisable link with the photo opposite is the Cotton Street cottages to the left, just glimpsed in the 1963 scene. Middle Street was realigned and rather than going alongside this end of the cottages it was diverted around the other side to rejoin itself at the rear. The opportunity was taken to form a short pedestrianised run from Cotton Street and under the archway. The latter had been removed from Woodhead's shop in the Market Place and connected the remaining rump of Middle Street with Cotton Street.

Market Place,
looking down
Station Road

To the left is what for a couple of generations of Bolsover folk was known as 'Wycherley's corner'. Harold Wycherley's chemist shop was later owned by John Mountain who maintained the shop name as it was well known, tried and tested. To the right a wagon unloads at Anne Woodhouse's grocery and on the same side can be seen the pebble dashed double frontage of the 1950's Coop Furnishing Store. Note the parked 'Baby Austin'.

Wycherley's corner now housing 'Oasis Florist's' has been restored and refurbished with its original stonework exposed and Georgian sashes replacing Wycherley's 1950's 'modernisation'. The restoration was submitted by Bolsover Civic Society for a National Civic Trust award and justifiably received a commendation.

The White Swan remains unchanged while the demolished Coop Furnishing has been replaced with the Pizza Takeaway, a concept unknown in Britain of the 1950's.

New Bolsover village green

A total of 194 houses were built in addition to a school cum village hall, institute, stores, Methodist chapel, and orphanage, plus sports facilities and allotment grounds. In concept, the scheme was an unusual one for a mining company to embark upon, in an industry which depends on limited reserves of natural materials, giving it a transient and insecure existence in one area.

Echoing other model villages such as Saltaire, Port Sunlight and Birmingham's Bournville, New Bolsover was the creation of Emerson Bainbridge, a Sheffield based industrialist, mining engineer, businessman and founder of the Bolsover Colliery Company. Bainbridge's vision for a workers model village was based on his nonconformist Liberal belief of a well housed workforce being key to a successful industry.

The large central green, planted with trees shrubs and flower beds, provided a focal point to the village. Houses were predominantly three bedroomed with a small number of two and four bedroomed ones. Rents varied around the three shillings a week mark. Tenants were carefully selected and anti social behaviour not permitted.

Here we see the village groundsman together with smartly dressed youngsters straight out of 'The Railway Children'.

Flower beds have gone but the shrubberies were replanted in the 1980's when the Green was refurbished and a children's' playground erected. The avenues of magnificent limes shroud the cottages in summer and it is still possible to be impressed by Bainbridge's vision, with its good quality accommodation and facilities in an industry which at the time usually provided the worst sort of workers housing.

The Green itself was generously proportioned and if the urban rows appear a little rigid for such a rural site the sudden appearance of New Bolsover, nestling beneath the enormous dramatic presence of Bolsover castle, never fails to impress.

D.H. Lawrence depicted the village as 'Stacks Gate' in 'Lady Chatterley's Lover'.

89

St Mary's House and school, Castle Street

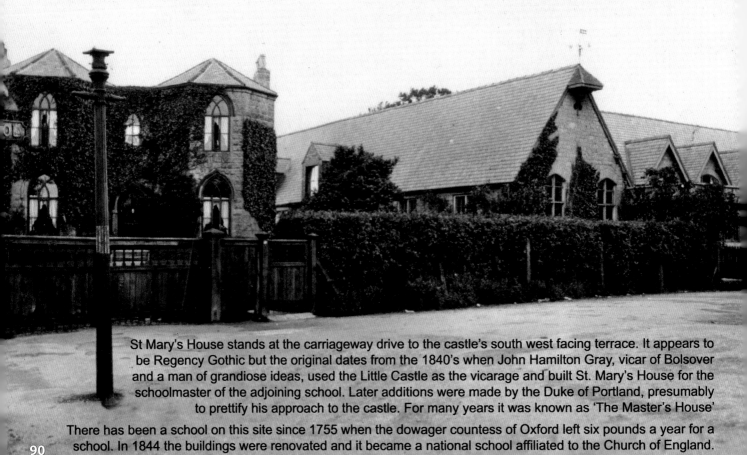

St Mary's House stands at the carriageway drive to the castle's south west facing terrace. It appears to be Regency Gothic but the original dates from the 1840's when John Hamilton Gray, vicar of Bolsover and a man of grandiose ideas, used the Little Castle as the vicarage and built St. Mary's House for the schoolmaster of the adjoining school. Later additions were made by the Duke of Portland, presumably to prettify his approach to the castle. For many years it was known as 'The Master's House'

There has been a school on this site since 1755 when the dowager countess of Oxford left six pounds a year for a school. In 1844 the buildings were renovated and it became a national school affiliated to the Church of England.

Today, St Mary's House hides behind a lush planting of trees so that in summer its fine appearance is unfortunately lost to the street.

In 1868 the school buildings, today Bolsover adult education centre, were rebuilt to what we see here, a pleasing range of local stone gables. By 1910 and the arrival of the colliery the building was catering for a vastly increased number of children, although New Bolsover took a large part of these with the new infant and elementary schools serving that village and Carr Vale. The 1903 inspectors report on the Castle Street school found almost seven hundred children on the roll in accommodation planned for half that number.

In 1910 the school was virtually rebuilt in red brick. Fortunately, the mid nineteenth century range was retained.

High Street

Taken from the top of Castle Lane this zig zag row of cottages ran along High Street towards Cotton Street. A mixture of rough cast older properties and later Victorian ones with dressed stone frontages they pre date the colliery.

It appears to be a beautifully sunny day with parlour blinds drawn against the westerly sun, a little lad gutter sitting and a couple of elegant perambulators in evidence. The dog with its arched back does not seem a fan of the photographer.

Today, a more open feeling is generated by the well landscaped car park and the single storey buildings housing the Royal Mail sorting office and Bolsover Family Centre. The twin brick gables of the old Presbyterian chapel stand proud.

It is fitting that a cyclist is passing the site of the cottage which in the earlier scene housed 'Hill's Cycle Workshop.'

Hockley from the Brek

An early 1950's view of Hockley towards Hill Top as Station Road sweeps into the Market Place. To the left, the old police station dominates the scene where basement cells were a natural attraction to local children. The Assembly Hall, Black Bull and White Swan are recognisable.

Cow Tail Row in the lower foreground has gone and the area has the feel of so many urban post war scenes. Whether due to aerial bombardment, the gloom and shabbiness of the early post war years or slum clearance, the pock marked result was the same.

A greener, more spruced up Hockley. The Assembly Hall, built in 1866 as the second home to Methodism in the town, with seating for two hundred people, has been transformed into the Assembly Hall and Community Centre, with two halls and assorted meeting rooms. Its glass extension harmonises well with the Victorian original and provides much needed community facilities to the town. The Bull has also been extended and refurbished since the previous scene, taking in the adjacent cottage.

The green space replacing Cow Tail Row provides a pleasant spacious feel to the Market Place approach.

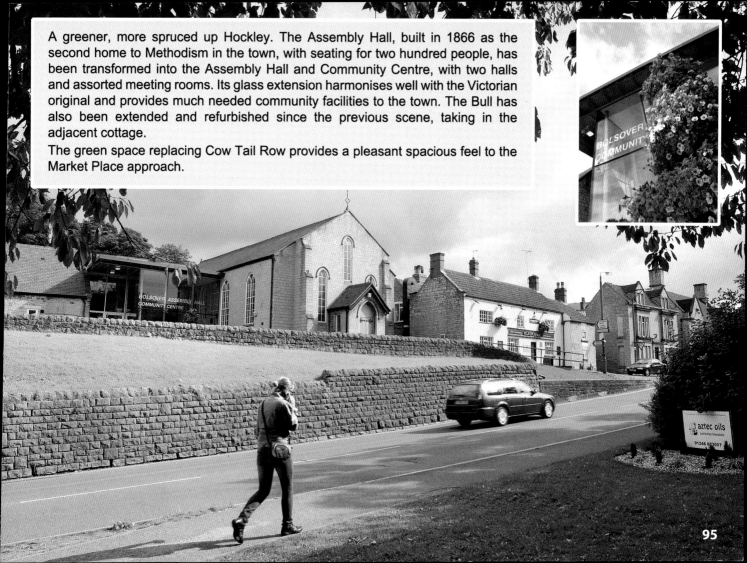

New Bolsover Stores and 'tub railway'

The tub railway ran from the colliery to the model village and round the backs of each cottage. Initially it carried bricks from the colliery brick yard to build the houses, later carrying the 'allowance coal' to each family and removing the waste from the middins sited at the bottom of each yard. Night soil man Sam Brassington remembers the smell as being 'pretty foul', possibly an understatement! The tubs ran on metal lines pulled by a horse.

The Stores, managed by the Company, was the only shop in the village and had separate departments for boots, groceries, drapery and butchery. It was planned on the assumption that there would be two hundred trading members, the number of families in the village and it held a virtual monopoly of trade within New Bolsover. Each family was expected to take out at least a one pound share in the Coop which included a piggery.

With its Victorian/Tudor timber framing, oriel windows and hanging first floor bays it remains a handsome building today, converted sympathetically to residential purposes. Internally, it has a central hall and two large rooms above but only the Victorian staircase remains.

The north gable end seen here is virtually unchanged.

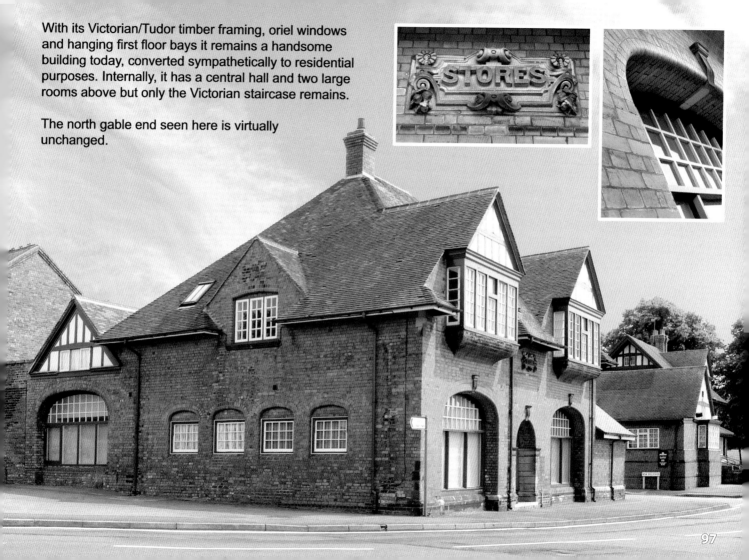

Town End

To the right there has been surprisingly little change since this photo was taken in the early 1950's.

Left, the white gable ended house, with the bulk of the Plaza cinema looming behind, has vanished, but everything else is much as it was.

More traffic, including lights and a less sleepy appearance here. The old lodging house to the immediate left is now a private house and the Plaza has been replaced by the Coop supermarket.

To the right the Beehive drapery façade has vanished behind the canopy projection of the chemist.

Sutton Hall

The Hall to the east and taken when the Arkwright family were in residence with gardeners to manage the grounds.

Built in 1724 to the designs of Frances Smith of Warwick for Nicholas Leake, last Earl of Scarsdale, the house in 1824 passed into the hands of the Arkwright family, descendents of Richard Arkwright, inventor and industrialist. Sold shortly after World War I, at a time when few people could afford the upkeep of such a property, it was bought by a speculator who sold anything he could, including internal panelling to the Philadelphia Museum of Modern Art.

Saved from total destruction by Sir Osbert Sitwell this magnificent pile now rests with English Heritage.

A gaunt and roofless ruin is the scene today with roof open to the sky and the lifeless window arches absorbing the mid morning sun. A car park replaces the grounds of the inhabited hall with the remaining greenery adopting the clinically spruce English Heritage look.

Acknowledgements

John Middleton whose black and white photographs form such an important part as the basis to this collection. Derbyshire Library Service, Bolsover Civic Society, children and staff of Bolsover Church of England Junior School and all those residents, householders and retailers who let Geoff and I enter gardens, climb walls and trees and were willing to pose or repeatedly walk up and down various streets until the shot was right.

Thanks are also due to Dennis Skinner MP who so readily agreed to write the foreword, a man who for forty years has strived to protect and improve the lives of local people and ensured the country at large is aware of the town's existence.

As usual, I need to thank my wife Jeanette for ensuring I was allowed time to do the work.

Photographs available to buy

Most of the images you see in this book are available to purchase as single prints, or produced on canvas at various sizes. Details at www.2ndimage.co.uk/bolsover

Further titles by Bernard Haigh

Bolsover Remembered
More Bolsover Remembered
One hundred years of mining: Bolsover colliery 1889-1989, a centenary history
Around Bolsover in old photographs
Bolsover Voices
Bolsover Town Trail
New Bolsover Trail

How well do you know Bolsover?

Throughout this book various pages have photographs inserted of features relating to the scene on that particular page. How many do you recognise? Page numbers are given with the answers below.

Bernard Haigh

Bernard has compiled many books on Bolsover and was commissioned by British Coal to write the centenary history of Bolsover colliery. A chartered librarian he has worked in libraries in Yorkshire, Birmingham and Derbyshire. He was Group Librarian, Bolsover and later Assistant City Librarian for Derby City Council. In 1979 he became a founder member of Bolsover Civic Society and remains its Secretary.

Geoff Harris

Geoff is a professional photographer. His business, 2nd Image Photography, provides commissioned images for local and national clients from his studio based in North West Lancashire. His work has been published in various books, a wide variety of magazines, websites and advertising material. He is an Associate of the British Institute of Professional Photography and is married with two children.